Published by Orange Hat Publishing 2023
ISBN: 9781645385318

Copyrighted © 2023 by Anne Lingelbach
All Rights Reserved
Birds on a Wire
Written by Anne Lingelbach
Illustrated by Haley Schulz

This publication and all contents within may not be reproduced or transmitted in any part or in its entirety without the written permission of the author.

www.orangehatpublishing.com

Written in honor
of the **songbirds** that
visit my backyard.

Baltimore oriole
Orange, sturdy
Whistling, clambering, darting
Acrobatic forager
Firebird

Black-capped chickadee
Tiny, inquisitive
Shivering, stashing, mobbing
Hops on trees
Blackcap raspberry

Cardinal
Red, regal
Singing, singing, singing
Symbolizes nearness of departed loved ones
King

Dark-eyed junco
Cute, pudgy
Hopping, fluttering, trilling
Travels in flocks
Snowbird

Goldfinch
Buttery, small
Dashing, undulating, chirping

House finch
Perky, stout
Bouncing, socializing, adapting
Feather colors determined by diet
Linnet

Pine siskin
Joyful, small
Twittering, fluttering, clinging
Temporarily stores seeds in its crop
Pine finch

Purple finch
Chunky, noisy
Warbling, chomping, dancing
Raspberry-colored feathers
American rose finch

Red-winged blackbird
Bold, stocky
Burbling, rambling, attention-seeking
Signals spring
Redwing

Robin
Large, industrious
Hopping, running, caroling
People-friendly personality
Red breast

Scarlet tanager
Stocky, social
Skulking, migrating, searching
Small and brightly colored
Redbird

Song sparrow
Adorable, bulky
Flitting, fluttering, serenading
Huge song playlist
Little brown job

Wren
Tiny, plump
Zipping, bouncing, scavenging
Feisty, bubbly songster
Imp

BIRD WATCHING

**Everyone can become a "birder."
All you need is a curious, patient attitude and a few tools.**

The **TOOLS** that you will need are:
- A bird book arranged by color
- A journal to record what you see
- Pencils (plain and colored)
- Binoculars

Identifying a bird is like solving a mystery. You become a detective, gathering clues. Sometimes you only need one or two clues to find an answer.

Ask yourself these **QUESTIONS** to help you identify a bird:
- What color is the bird?
- Does it have field marks (stripes or dots)?
- How big is it?
- Where did you see it?
- What was the bird doing?
- What sounds did it make?

Record your findings and make a sketch of the bird in your journal. There are many websites and apps to help you learn about birds. Perhaps when you have learned about some birds, you will want to write your own cinquain poems!

ANIMAL CINQUAIN GUIDELINES

LINE ONE: Animal's name

LINE TWO: Two adjectives describing the animal

LINE THERE: Three action words that end in "ing"

LINE FOUR: A short phrase about the animal

LINE FIVE: Another name or word for the animal